The Canary
Companion Cook Book

Jacqueline T. Moore

ALL RIGHTS RESERVED

No part of this book may be reproduced or transmitted in any form or by any means, electronic or mechanical, including photocopying, recording, or by any information storage and retrieval system, without permission in writing from the author, except in the case of brief quotations embodied in reviews.

Publisher's Note:

This is a work of fiction. All names, characters, places, and events are the work of the author's imagination.

Any resemblance to real persons, places, or events is coincidental.

Solstice Publishing -
www.solsticepublishing.com

Copyright 2018 – Jacqueline T. Moore

The Canary Companion Cookbook

Jacqueline T. Moore

For Kenneth P. Jacobs, the inspiration for this collection.

Table of Contents

6 – 18	**Beverages**
19 – 29	**Bread & Jam**
30 – 42	**Beans & Grains & Noodles**
43 – 58	**Cakes & Toppings**
59 – 73	**Fruits & Vegetables**
74 – 90	**Cookies & Puddings & Cobblers & Pies**
91 – 103	**Soups & Stews**
104 – 129	**Meat & Fish & Eggs**

Beverages

Boiled Coffee (Jamoke)
Found in *The Canary*, *The Checkerboard*, *The Cornerpost*

The old method of boiling coffee is still practiced by approximately one-half of the housekeepers in this country. The coffee is sometimes boiled with an egg, which makes it perfectly clear, and also enriches it. When an egg is not used a small piece of salt fish skin is boiled with the coffee to clear it.

Ingredients
1 small cupful of roasted and ground coffee beans (⅓ Mocha and ⅔ Java)
1 small egg, shell and all, broken into the pot with the dry coffee

Instructions
Stir grounds and egg well in coffee pot. Pour three pints of boiling water over it. Boil for five to ten minutes, counting from the time it begins to bubble.

After boiling, pour in a cupful of cold water. Pour a little of the coffee into a cup to ensure the nozzle of the pot is not filled with grounds. Pour this back, and let the coffee stand a few moments to settle, taking care that it does not boil again.

The advantages of boiled coffee are many. When the egg is used, the yolk gives a very rich flavor, and when milk or cream is added, the coffee has a pleasing, rich, yellow look. It has also a peculiar flavor, which many people prefer to the flavor gained by any other process.

One disadvantage to this method of coffee making is that the egg coats the dry coffee. When the hot water is added to the mixture, the coating becomes hard and a great deal of the best of the coffee remains in the grounds after boiling. Also, in boiling, much of the fine flavor is lost in the steam that escapes from the pot.

Adapted from *Miss Parloa's New Cook Book (1880)*

The Canary
Boiled Coffee

Clarisse knew the best thing for the situation was to boil some coffee. As quick as she could get the eggshell in, the cups were poured. Jack drank, sitting quietly, looking from face to face. He knew that, right then, he was safe. He also knew the woman had kissed him as she mended him. That, he kept in his heart. After Clarisse had served up some pot roast with gravy bread, he felt he could move. Maude brought down his oldest shirt for Jack. The two sailors thanked their new-found friends and headed to the ship. As they walked, Sure Foot told Jack everything.

The Checkerboard
Boiled Coffee

Captain Calhoun was dead drunk. Must have been since one bell. CB knew because he served the brandy. Captain always had drink on his dinner tray.
"Sir?" CB shook the captain's shoulder. "Sir, time for charts, we gotta get to work." Captain Calhoun snorted, but did not lift his head. "Come on, sir, we need to work."
The captain opened one eye, the one buried in his arm.
"Hush boy. Can't you see it's night?"
CB gave him another shake. "Open your other eye, sir. It's day."

"Damn." Captain was not one to swear sober. "Damn."

"I'll get coffee from Cookie. We gotta do charts, or tiller man will drive us who-knows-where."

"No coffee, brandy," argued Captain, closing his free eye.

The Cornerpost
Boiled Coffee

"Cold milk and crackers? You're feeding our children cold milk and crackers?" Myra stared at her husband.

CB stood at the sleeping porch's door with a tray of milk, crackers, and coffee. "Sorry, Cookie never taught us about kitchens. At least they said grace. Junior changed 'Father, thank you for this food, to 'Father, bless CB for marrying our mama'. I'm guessin' what we had wasn't really food, and the boy was standin' up for me the best he could." He held out their supper. Marguerite took the offering with a scowl.

Hot Punch or Tonic
Found in *The Cornerpost*

Ingredients
½ pint of rum
½ pint of brandy
¼ pound of sugar
1 large lemon, juiced
½ teaspoonful of nutmeg
1 pint of boiling water

Instructions
Rub the sugar over the lemon until it has absorbed all the yellow part of the skin, and then put the sugar into a punchbowl. Squeeze the lemon over a strainer to catch the pips. Add the lemon-juice to the sugar. Mix these two ingredients well together. Pour in the boiling water over them, stirring well together. Add the rum, brandy, and nutmeg, mixing thoroughly. The punch is ready to serve.

When making a good punch, it is very important that all the ingredients are thoroughly incorporated; and, to insure success, the processes of mixing must be diligently attended to.

Sufficient: Allow a quart for 4 persons; but this information must be taken *cum grano salis*, for the capacities for this kind of beverage are generally supposed to vary considerably for each person.

From *The Book of Household Management (1861)*

The Cornerpost
Hot Tonic

"Auntie, you tellin' me the lemonade's spiked? I didn't know you drank spirits."
"Shush, child, don't be shocked. You can't tell me you haven't had a hot tonic before?"
Myra smiled. "Yes, ma'am, I have. Guess we can call the lemonade cold tonic."

Tea and Fruit Punch
(Methodist Ladies Punch)
Found in *The Cornerpost*

Ingredients
2 tablespoons black loose tea leaves
2 cups sugar
½ cup orange juice
4 lemons
3 oranges
4 cups ginger beer
2 cups water

Instructions
Boil the water. Add the tea and sugar. Let stand for thirty seconds, and then strain. Add orange juice and the juice of the lemons. Add the oranges, thinly sliced, and the ginger beer. Pour over 8 cups of ice in a punch bowl.

Adapted from an old family recipe

The Cornerpost
Tea and Fruit Punch
(Methodist Ladies Punch)

Ada tasted her lemonade. "Darn, this is Methodist tea punch. Please see if there is another pitcher in there somewhere."

Tea

Found in *The Checkerboard* and *The Cornerpost*

Ingredients
4 tablespoons black loose tea leaves
4 cups water
Milk to taste
Sugar to taste
Lemon and honey if desired

Instructions
In making tea, the following rules should be observed:

The water should be freshly boiled.
The teapot, which should be of earthen or china (never of tin), should be scalded and heated before putting in the tea.

Pour on the boiling water and cover closely, and let stand for 3 or 4 minutes before using. Never, under any circumstances, allow tea to boil. The usual proportion is a small teaspoonful of tea to 1 cup of boiling water, but this is too strong for general use.

From *Public School Domestic Science (1898)*
#5 Vanilla Sugar
Found in *The Checkerboard* and *The Cornerpost*

Ingredients
1 ounce of dried vanilla beans
½ pound of granulated sugar

Instructions
Cut the dried vanilla beans into pieces and use a pestle to crush them in a mortar with the granulated sugar to a fine powder. Pass it through a fine sieve. Crush again the coarse pieces that do not go through the sieve the first time. Store in a well-corked bottle or preserve jar.

Adapted from *The Century Cook Book (1901)*

The Checkerboard
Tea with Vanilla Sugar and Best Cream

They watched as she stepped into the first tea room she could find. *Princesses drink tea.*

Two steps in and she was stopped by a frilly aproned white woman, holding a painted china pot. "Girl." The painted pot holder barely spoke through her tight lips. "You are in a ladies' tea room," she sniffed.

"I know."

"This is no place for colored."

"Madam, I am Princess Lulah Marie Dubonet, and today is my birthday." She walked past the woman into a room of staring tea drinkers. She sat at a small table near the sideboard, and smoothed an invisible crumb off the doily. "You may serve me now. Do not forget your best cream."

This time, painted pot holder opened her mouth. "Girl, I don't care if you are the queen of Araby, you are not welcome here. Leave now."

"And two vanilla sugar lumps. Don't make me wait." Lulah Marie was very used to getting exactly what she wanted. She had no patience for truck like this.

"Get out or I will use the telephone and call the sheriff."

Bread & Jam

Baking Powder Biscuits
Found in *The Cornerpost*

Ingredients
2 pints of flour
Butter the size of an egg
3 heaping teaspoonfuls of baking powder
1 teaspoonful of salt

Instructions
Make a soft dough of sweet milk or water, kneading as little as possible. Cut out with the usual biscuit-cutter and bake in an oven heated to 400 degrees.

Adapted from *The White House Cook Book (1887)*

The Cornerpost
Baking Powder Biscuits

(Author's note: Biscuits are in all three books. This passage is one of my favorites.)

Jack nodded, licking his lips. "Good." He stepped up to the stove. "I'll start the meat if you mix the biscuits."
Using a drinking glass, she rolled the dough and cut the circles. "Oh, *mon amour*, why can't we have our own house?"
"Huh?" Jack didn't hear her soft words above the sizzle of the frying ham. "What?"
"I'm tired of not having my own kitchen." She sniffled. "I want my own house." Marguerite swiped away the tears that had just begun, leaving a smear of flour on her cheek.
"We're set up good. I have the ship, and you live with Myra. Don't need to change." Jack looked at the rising biscuits. "How soon?"
"Maybe never," she whispered.

Breakfast Honey Rolls
Found in *The Cornerpost*

Ingredients
½ pound of flour
1 heaping teaspoonful of baking powder
1 level teaspoonful of salt
1 heaping teaspoonful of sugar
1 ounce of lard
Cold milk
1 cup honey

Instructions
Mix well by sifting together the flour, baking powder, salt, and sugar. Rub a little of the mixture into the lard, and then mix it with the rest of the flour. Quickly wet it up with enough cold milk to enable you to roll it out about half an inch thick. Cut out the dough with a tin shape or with a sharp knife, in the form of diamonds. Lightly wet the top with water, and double them half over. Put them upon a tin, buttered and warmed, and bake them in a hot oven (400-425 degrees). When done, set out on plate and pour good honey over them.

Adapted from *Twenty-Five Cent Dinners for Families of Six (1879)*.

The Cornerpost
Breakfast Honey Rolls

"Maybe someday..." Isaac glanced at their house. "Oh gosh, look. She's back." He quick-stepped it to the porch.

Louise collected Ikey in her arms. "Good to see you, son." Circling his shoulder, she guided him into the parlor, walking wide from Isaac. "I made honey rolls. Want one?"

"Just had pie, but yeah, smells good." Ikey smiled. "We missed you." He plopped in his spot.

Isaac hung his bowler and followed the two into the kitchen, sitting at his own place. "Hello, Louise. How are you?"

"Hello. I'm well." She poured him a fresh mug.

Suddenly Isaac felt bashful. "How was your visit?"

"I did everything I set out to do." She put the delightfully drippy rolls in front of them. "I know you like honey." She wiped the edge of the plate, scooping up the stray sauce, and licked her finger clean. "This is good."

Hot Water Cornbread

Found in *The Checkerboard*

Ingredients
1 tablespoon lard (Cookie used bacon grease)
¾ cup boiling water
1 cup corn meal
1 teaspoon salt

Instructions
Mix all ingredients until it feels somewhat like smooth mashed potatoes. Heat more bacon grease in large skillet until medium hot, but not smoking. Gently drop a heaping spoonful of cornmeal mix in hot grease and flatten with back of spoon. Do a few more.

Cook until they are brown on the bottom and then flip. Take out of grease when that side is brown. Drain and serve hot. Keep making more. Be sure to eat one yourself, because there won't be any left when you are done.

Adapted from the Smith Family recipe

The Checkerboard
Hot Water Cornbread

Jack had the jitters. Today was his first docking and roll off since he became Chief.
"You nervous?" Cookie was keeping an early Jack in the galley for breakfast. "Don't want him to hear all that dirt the men are talking," he muttered quietly over the pot of boiling water soon to be turned into grits.
"I can't make any mistakes today." Jack had heard Cookie's words. "You know, they'll be watching everything I do."
"I know."
"Not only our crew, but as soon as the dock men hear that the *Sallie* has a colored Chief, they're gonna be like flies on manure lookin' to fault me." Jack glanced around the galley. "Any yesterday cornbread? Don't think I can wait for the cooking."
"You can wait, and yes, there're a few cuts in the box. Get me a piece, too."

F.R.O.G Jam

Found in *The Cornerpost*
F.R.O.G. JAM
(Figs, Raspberries, Orange, Ginger)

Ingredients
5 cups dried figs, remove stems and quarter
2 cups orange juice
1 ½ cups raspberries
1 Tbsp freshly grated ginger
1 cup sugar (more or less to taste)

Instructions
In a large pot add figs and orange juice. Bring to a boil, then reduce heat to a simmer and cover. Cook until skins are soft and the seeds are loose (about 15 minutes), stirring every few minutes. Add raspberries and ginger. Increase heat to medium and stir frequently. Cook until the raspberries have fallen apart and are well incorporated. Mash with potato masher until somewhat smooth. Add sugar to taste. Canning method: water bath
Makes 5 to 6 (8 oz) jars

Adapted from the Jacobs Family recipe

The Cornerpost
F.R.O.G Jam

As Isaac called "Good bye, everyone" from the front door, Ikey asked for more toast. "You Reform like the Cohens and my father? I was raised Methodist."

Louise smeared the bread with a thick layer of the F.R.O.G. jam she'd brought in with her. "Does that mean you say grace?"

"Only when someone's listening." He finished his glass of milk. "My mother listened."

Louise sat across the table, opposite from where Isaac left his mug. "Do you want me to?"

"Naw."

"Your dinner pail's ready. When you get home, tell me what you didn't like. That way I'll not pack it again."

"Miss Louise, I really like ham and cheese. Father said we can't buy anything piggy to eat." He looked up at her with the slightest frown. "Would it be wrong if *you* bought sliced ham, and hid it in the back of the icebox? Father doesn't need to know."

"You little stinker." Louise gathered his breakfast plate and handed him his bucket. "I know Jewish families don't eat pork. If I recall, you said that you are Methodist. Don't see why you can't have what *you* want." Laying her hand on his shoulder, she winked. "Our little secret?"

"Oh, yes, ma'am, our little secret."

Bitter Orange Marmalade
Found in *The Canary*

Ingredients
12 bitter oranges
3 sweet oranges
3 lemons
White sugar

Instructions
Slice or shave the bitter oranges and lemons very thin, laying aside the pips in a bowl; pare or slice the sweet oranges.

To every pint of fruit add four pints cold water. Cover the pips with water and let stand for twenty-four hours.

Boil until the pips are quite tender, then place in a muslin bag when ready. To every pound of fruit add one and one half pounds white sugar. Include the bag of pips and boil until it jellies, from twenty to thirty minutes.

Attributed to Mrs. R. Stewart, *My Pet Recipes, Tried and True (1900)*

The Canary
Bitter Orange Marmalade

"Um, just making conversation." Julia thought fast. "The ladies of the Guild were talking about the results of rickets just the other day." She handed him the butter dish. "Care for jam?" She knew he did not like marmalade, so she passed that pot first.

Beans & Grains & Noodles

Dry Beans to Boil

Found in *The Canary*

Ingredients
2 cups dry pinto beans, washed and sorted
2-3 quarts water

Instructions
Put the beans in a saucepan with 2 quarts cold water, and boil gently till tender. If the water boils away, fill up with another quart cold water. Never put any salt to boil dry beans, it prevents them from cooking. As soon as boiled tender, drain them, and they are ready for use. Add salt to taste.

Adapted from *Hand-Book of Practical Cookery (1884)*

The Canary
Dry Beans to Boil

Myra tied on her black bonnet, grabbed up her loaded basket, and stepped out on the porch, pushing the screen shut. She knew Junior wanted a break and did not have to have this man telling her so. Shoot, *she* needed a break! She adjusted her load and looked up at the Principal.
"Let's go toward the store. Sometimes they can trick my uncle into thinkin' it's a day off." Harry always kept rice and beans stewing in the back. Any hungry man coming to the side door could have a meal, just for the asking. To treat the little ones he would dish out a plate of rice, pour some sweet molasses over it, and the children would be in heaven. Myra knew that Aunt Ada would have shooed them off to school by now, so today must be Guild. If they were at the store, Uncle Harry would have his hands full. She stepped up her pace.

Cookie's Grits
Found in *The Checkerboard*

Ingredients
3 cups water
1 cup grits
1 teaspoon salt

Instructions
Get your water boiling hard. Add salt. Keep the boil. Slowly stir grits into the water, keeping the water moving. When all the grits are in the boil, start whipping the mix. Don't stop. Whip 'til your fork don't move. You're done. Mash in lots of butter.

Adapted from an old family recipe.

The Checkerboard
Cookie's Grits

Junior found Black Jack at breakfast mess. "Liar, liar, pants on fire, damn it, Mister Jack." He slammed his kit on the closest table and ran head first into Jack's chest. "Liar, liar, liar," the boy yelled. Junior locked his arms around the man and butted him like a Billy goat. The hall went dead silent. The men watched the skinny, but strong grandson of a slave calmly raise the boy by his elbows and drop him to the floor. Then he scooped up the stunned prisoner, threw him over his shoulder, and nodded to his audience. "Men, I'll take care of this little problem. Y'all enjoy your grits. Hope Chief doesn't shackle him."

Boiled Rice

Found in *The Cornerpost*

Ingredients
2 cups white long grain rice
10 cups water
1 tablespoon salt

Instructions
Pick your rice clean, and wash it in two cold waters, not draining off the last water till you are ready to put the rice on the fire. Prepare a saucepan of water with a little salt in it, and when it boils, sprinkle in the rice.

Boil it hard twenty minutes, keeping it covered. Then take it from the fire, and pour off the water.

Afterwards set the saucepan in the chimney corner (a warm spot on the stove off of direct heat) with the lid off, while you are dishing your dinner, to allow the rice to dry, and the grains to separate.

Rice, if properly boiled, should be soft and white, and every grain ought to stand alone. If badly managed, it will, when brought to table, be a grayish watery mass.

In most southern families, rice, is boiled every day for the dinner table, and eaten with the meat and poultry.

From *Directions for Cookery, in its Various Branches (1840).*

The Cornerpost
Boiled Rice

Yes, Linda Sue sure did set those hornets to work. They circled Ada all the walk home, and kept swarming in the kitchen. "How can they find anything to talk about our Myra? She's better off than most since she got married." Ada was getting out the Sunday dinner china, grumping and mumbling. "Harry, darlin', would you see if the rice has set up?"

"Only if you tell me what happened in church. You're really out of sorts."

"Linda Sue."

Harry peeked under the rice pot's lid. The starch was still floating. "I'm a'guessin' another ten minutes. Want me to stir it?"

"Don't touch it 'til the holes bubble."

"Yes, ma'am." Harry settled into his spot at the table. "What about Linda Sue? She's not one to rile you like this."

Breakfast Rice for Six Persons
Found in *The Checkerboard*

Ingredients
1 pound of Patna rice
2 ounces of butter
2 quarts of water
A small bit of cinnamon or lemon-peel
Salt
3 pints of skim milk
Honey or sugar

Instructions
Put the rice into a boiling pot with the butter, water, cinnamon or lemon-peel, and a little salt. Put the lid on, and set the rice to boil very gently indeed close to the the warming plate at the back of the stove. Leave until the rice is done quite soft; this will take about one hour and a quarter. Add the skim milk, and after having stirred the rice-milk over the fire for ten minutes longer, it may be sweetened with a little honey or sugar, and will produce an excellent breakfast for at least six persons.

Adapted from *A Plain Cookery Book for the Working Classes (1852)*

The Checkerboard
Breakfast Rice for Six Persons

Aunt Ada cooked them whatever they wanted to eat and the boys were allowed to choose the best marbles in the case. Uncle Harry gave Junior his full dinner hour to play. Both chose ham and cheese sandwiches with left over breakfast rice mixed with sugar and cream for dessert.

Ada smiled at Ikey. "Missing good old food?" was all she said as she handed the boys their plates.

"Yes'm."

"Let me know if you want more."

"Yes'm." Ikey blew Ada a little kiss as a thank you. "You know I will."

After several sandwiches and two bowls of creamy rice washed down with big glasses of milk, Junior led them back into the storage room to play. This is where he slept. Stock wasn't too high to cover the windows, and they were out from under foot and away from the grown-ups.

Fried Noodles
Found in *The Cornerpost*

Ingredients
3 whole eggs
Flour
Butter
1 cup of milk

Instructions
Beat eggs very light and sift in sufficient flour to make a stiff paste. Work until smooth.

Break off a piece and roll out on board very thin. Break off another piece and repeat until all the dough is used.

Let rolled-out dough dry, then cut all except one piece into long strips one inch wide. Fold the one last piece in layers and cut into very fine noodles.

Boil large noodles in pot of salted boiling water. When the noodles are tender, drain in colander and pour into baking dish. Stir in two tablespoons of butter.

Heat a tablespoon of butter in the frying-pan and brown fine noodles in this butter. Sprinkle these over the broad noodles; pour milk over the whole and brown in 400 degree oven. Serve in same dish in which it was baked.

Adapted from *The International Jewish Cook Book (1919)*

(Author's note: Esther used schmaltz, chicken fat, instead of butter.)

The Cornerpost
Fried Noodles

Esther drained the broth and fat into a bowl and set in the cool root cellar. Pulling the meat off the skin and bones, she put that it in the icebox for later. Unfortunately the noodle dough had been drying a bit too long to make good cuts, so she did the best she could with the wettest parts.

When the *schmaltz* was floating, perfect for lifting, Esther spooned that delicious fat into her skillet for the frying. She poured all that wonderful broth back into the pot. Soon it was ready. Her husband liked his noodles boiled soft and fried softer.

Cakes & Toppings

Angel Food Cake
Found in *The Cornerpost*

Ingredients
1 tumbler of flour (1 cup)
1 teaspoonful of cream of tartar
1 ½ tumblers of white powdered sugar (1 ¾ cup)
Whites of 11 eggs
3 teaspoonfuls of vanilla extract

Instructions
Mix flour, powdered sugar, and cream of tartar, then sift it five times.

Beat the egg whites into a stiff froth, then stir the sugar into the eggs by degrees, very lightly and carefully. Gently add vanilla extract.

After this, add the flour, stirring quickly and lightly. Pour it into a clean, bright tin cake-dish, which should not be buttered or lined.

Bake at once in a moderate (375 degrees) oven about forty minutes, testing it with a broom splint.

When done, let it remain in the cake-tin, turning it upside down, with the sides resting on the tops of two saucers so that a current of air will pass under and over it.

Adapted from *The White House Cook Book (1887)*

(Author's note: I remember my mother setting the cake pan up-side-down on a Coca Cola bottle to cool.)

The Cornerpost
Angel Food Cake

Louise looked at her growing stack of supplies. "Was his wife a simple cook?"
"Oh, Lord no. Julia, rest her soul, was a fantastic cook. She made the most wonderful angel food cake with orange sauce." Ada licked her lips. "I could eat a slice right this very minute."
"I'll have to learn."
Ada looked at Louise. "Where's your grocery tote? I thought all Jewish women used them."
"I, uh, didn't notice if there was one in the house. Could you box this up for me? I would appreciate it so much."
"Of course." Ada started packing one of the small wooden crates by the counter. "Now, I don't know what you're used to in Austin, but around here, it's expected that you bring it back next week. Makes it easier for those who forget."

Lemon Cake

Found in *The Canary*

Ingredients
Cake
½ cup of butter
1 ½ cups of sugar
3 eggs
1 cup of milk
2 teaspoonfuls of baking powder
3 cups of flour

Frosting
Grated rind of 1 lemon, and the juice of 2 lemons
¾ cup of sugar
2 egg whites

Instructions
Cake
Cream butter well with sugar, stir in the yolks of the eggs and the milk.

Sift baking powder with the flour and add alternately with the egg whites beaten into a stiff froth.

Bake about 45 minutes in rather a quick oven (375 degrees) in three tins of uniform size. Cool.

Frosting
Mix the lemon rind, juice, and sugar. Let boil and throw it over the well beaten whites of two eggs.

This cake is one that keeps well for five or six days.

Adapted from Miss Beemer *My Pet Recipes, Tried and True (1900)*

The Canary
Lemon Cake

Uncle Harry went straight upstairs when he got back to his store. The men were waiting, drinking coffee and eating the lemon cream cake that Ada had left on the steps. The Brothers were enjoying the telling of what they had done.
Everyone knew Rabbi Cohen was a tea drinker and he was well complemented on his drunk acting. Robearde had beat Harry to the lodge kitchen and had told them all about the swearing. Harry cut himself a slice, poured a cup, and joined in. The Masons had done their good deed for the day. They all agreed that operation Jail Bird was a roaring success.

Missus Annie's Pound Cake
Found in *The Checkerboard*

Ingredients
1 pound sugar (about 2 cups)
1 pound butter
1 pound flour (about 4 cups)
1 pound eggs (10-12 depending on size)
¼ teaspoon salt
½ teaspoon mace (Annie used nutmeg when she didn't have mace)

Instructions
Preheat oven 325 degrees. Butter and flour your pan. Annie used a tube pan because the cake had a nice crust all around and was easier to serve.

Sift together flour, salt, and mace. Set aside. Cream butter and sugar until well mixed. Slowly add dry ingredients, making sure everything is stirred in.

Pour into the pan and bake 1 hour 15 minutes, checking if center is done with a tester (toothpick).

Depending on your pan and your oven, you may need to bake an additional 15 minutes or more until tester is clean.

Adapted from a 1700's recipe.

The Checkerboard
Missus Annie's Pound Cake

He headed toward the hampers of food. "Excuse me, everyone, but I never ate my dinner." He turned to his wife. "Linda Sue, please join me. I don't believe you got dessert. Miss Annie, did you bring your wonderful pound cake?"

Annie smiled through her grief. "Yes, sir, I did. Let me cut it."

Justine, the newest guild member, was the first to notice the emerald and diamonds on Annie's left hand.

"Why, Miss Annie, what a lovely ring. Is it from your mother?" Justine realized what she said, and clapped her hand over her mouth. "Oh, Miss Annie, I'm sorry," she murmured through her fingers.

"No. It is my engagement ring."

The entire choir loft fell silent.

"Your, your what?" Justine stammered.

Miss Annie raised her voice. "My engagement ring. I am betrothed to Mr. Carlton Wilson."

"Father's friend?" her sisters shrieked in unison. The ladies of the guild stared.

"Yes, Father's friend." Annie's pinched lips spoke volumes. "We have been engaged for several years. We were waiting for the right time."

"Why didn't you tell us?" Emily stood by the stacks of practice hymnals, arms crossed.

"Don't you think your sister and I have a right to know?"
"Not really."

White Cake with Berries
Found in *The Checkerboard*

Ingredients
2 cups of sugar
¾ cup of butter
¾ cup of water
3 heaping cups of flour
6 egg whites3 teaspoons of baking powder
1 teaspoon of vanilla

Instructions
Beat sugar and butter to a cream, and then add water, flour, egg whites beaten to a stiff froth, baking powder, and vanilla. Bake in layer pans, and put together with frosting. Cover the top layer with fresh berries.

Attributed to Mrs. W. C. Butcher *Recipes Tried and True (1894)*

The Checkerboard
White Cake with Berries

"Nothing new. Most all the men worked hard. That Zico complained that his nose hurt too much for him to do much, but I pointed at Donneley and commented on how hard he was working and that since he'd broken his nose, Donneley's must hurt a whole heap more." Jack chuckled. "The fools started jaw-jackin' about who was the stronger, and next thing ya know, they finished their loading." He took a third slice of berry cake.

Yellow Cake
Found in *The Checkerboard*

Ingredients
¼ cup butter
½ cup sugar
5 egg yolks ½ cup milk
⅞ cup flour
1 teaspoons baking powder
1 teaspoon orange extract

Instructions
Cream the butter and add sugar gradually. Beat the egg yolks until thick and lemon colored, and add to the butter and sugar mixture. Add extract.

Mix and sift flour and baking powder, and add alternately with milk to first mixture.

Bake 350 degrees in a greased cake pan until golden. (You may omit the orange extract and add one-half cup nut-meat cut in small pieces, and bake in individual tins.

Adapted from *The Boston Cooking-School Cook Book (1896)*

(Author's note: This was served with a brown sugar drizzle made with one cup melted butter and one cup brown sugar, mixed and poured over the cake.)

The Checkerboard
Yellow Cake

Cookie raised his coffee mug to Jack. "Ya done good, boy." He cut the yellow one with the melted brown sugar drizzle. Jack smiled and took the offered first piece.
"Thank you, sir."

Cold Orange Sauce

Found in *The Cornerpost*

Ingredients
1 teacupful of butter
2 teacupfuls of fine white sugar
Grated rind of 1 orange and the juice of 2
Nutmeg

Instructions
Beat butter and sugar to a cream; then stir in the orange rind and juice. Stir until all the orange juice is absorbed. Grate nutmeg upon the sauce and serve on a flat dish.

From *The White House Cook Book (1887)*

The Cornerpost
Cold Orange Sauce

"Oh Auntie, what am I going to do? I never thought…"
"No, you didn't." Ada looked over at the cake in the dining room. "Right now you are going to cut me a slice. Do you have orange sauce?" The niece nodded. "We are going to enjoy it before the children turn into a swarm of angel food eating locusts," Ada continued. "Tonight, after I get my breath and the children are in bed, we will talk this out."
"Yes, ma'am. I am just so sorry."
"I know. Now cut the cake."

Fruits & Vegetables

Compote of Blackberries, Currants, Raspberries, Strawberries, and other like Berries

Found in *The Cornerpost*

Ingredients
2 pounds mixed berries
1 ¼ cups sugar
¾ cup water

Instructions
Prepare syrup by boiling sugar and water until approximately 230 degrees. Throw the berries in. Boil from one to five minutes, according to the kind of berries you use. Take from the fire when you see the berries start to open and release their juices. Serve when cold.

Adapted from *Hand-Book of Practical Cookery (1884)*

Gooseberries
Found in *The Cornerpost*

Ingredients
1 pound gooseberries
1 pound sugar
2 cups water

Instructions
Select young gooseberries. Make a syrup with one pound of loaf sugar to each of fruit; stew them till quite clear and the syrup becomes thick, but do not let them be mashed. Do not cover the pan while they are stewing.

(*Author's note:* They are excellent made into tarts.)

The Cornerpost
Berry Compote

"Husband, wait just a minute, this meal's not finished." Ada stood. She returned with a bowl of berry compote. Mixed in was a fruit Harry had never seen before. "Let me get the sauce dishes."

"Woman, what are those round green things? Never seen them before." Harry poked at one with his fork.

"Gooseberries. Susan brought me some from her yard. Said they're really hard to grow."

Harry honked. "I'm not a goose."

"Hush." Ada filled each bowl, and pointed the serving spoon at CB. "Go on with your idea."

CB popped a gooseberry in his mouth. "Yum, they're good." He eyed the bread and honey. "Now?"

"Serve your uncle first."

Jarred Peaches
Found in *The Canary*

Ingredients
1 measure peaches
¾ measure sugar
(*Author's note:* I adjusted this measure to 6 pounds peaches for 4 cups sugar and 5 cups water. Use pint jars.)

Instructions
The skin can easily be removed from peaches, leaving a smooth surface, by placing them in a wire basket and plunging it for a moment into 5 cups boiling water.

From the boil put the fruit into cold water and rinse it several times, then rub off the skin. Cut each peach in thick slices and place again in cold water to preserve the color until ready to use.

Place in a large pan 4 cups sugar.. Add a very little water to dissolve the sugar. Let it boil a minute, and add the boiling water used for the skins.

Then add as much fruit as will float without crowding, and cook until it is transparent, but not until it loses shape. Remove each piece separately as soon as it is cooked. Add the next pieces until all are cooked.

When ready to fill the jars, place them carefully in a pan of boiling water; have the tops and rubbers also in hot water.

Part of the fruit has become cooled while the rest was cooking, but, as it must go into the jars hot, place it again in the boiling syrup, a little at a time.

Use a ladle or cup to dip out the fruit; run a spoon-handle around the inside of the jars after they are filled to liberate any air bubbles.

Add enough syrup to fill them to overflowing, and adjust the rubber and top on each jar as it is filled. Any juice that is left over may be boiled down to a jelly, or it may be bottled to use as flavoring or for sauces.

Adapted from *The Century Cook Book (1901)*

The Canary
Jarred Peaches

Myra sniffled, breathed deep, and kissed her aunt. She had heard every word not spoken. Aunt Ada believed her and was planning to stay away overnight if needed. She ran into her room and got her money. She lined her bosom with the bills and wrapped her coins in a handkerchief, dropping it into one of her apron pockets. Opening her dress, she then took the Canary, blessed it with a kiss and laced it through her stays, securing it against her shimmy. After everything was back in place, she pinned the cameo to her throat. If worse came to worse, she could sell the jewelry. CB's packets of letters were under her mattress, tucked inside the ticking. Myra dropped them in the pocket besides her coins. "Heavenly Father, keep him safe from whatever this is," she prayed. She got everything off the three beds and the trundle and robbed the blanket safe, taking the winter quilts. She quickly tightened them into bedrolls and bound them with the string she wrapped her sweets.

Aunt Ada was packing the largest basket she could find with all the food she could scrounge up.

"Is there any room in your sweets basket?" she asked.

"'Bout half."

"See what you can do about your jarred peaches."

"Yes, Ma'am." Myra now knew for sure that Aunt Ada believed her, because those peaches were a sacred treat. No one in the family was ever allowed to open a jar of peaches until Christmas morning. The fruit would be shared out into everyone's breakfast bowls and then the jar would be passed to have a sip of the juice, like so much Communion. Even the babies would get drops on their tongues. Those peaches were the symbol of family. Now Aunt Ada wanted her to pack them in her basket. Maybe she was starting to smell the fear, too. Myra packed all six.

Baked Beets

Found in *The Canary*

Ingredients
2 beets per serving
Salt, pepper, butter to taste

Instructions
Beets retain their sugary, delicate flavor to perfection if they are baked instead of boiled. Turn them frequently while in the oven, using a knife, as the fork allows the juice to run out. When done remove the skin, and serve with butter, salt and pepper on the slices.

From *The White House Cook Book (1887)*

Beet Greens (Tops)
Found in *The Canary*

Ingredients
Tops from 2 or more beets per serving
1 teaspoon salt for boiling water
Salt, pepper, butter to taste

Instructions
Beets are usually thickly sowed, and as the young plants begin to grow they must be thinned out. These plants make delicious greens, and even the tops of the ordinary market beets are good if properly prepared. Examine the leaves carefully to be sure that there are no insects on them; wash thoroughly in several waters, and put over the fire in a large kettle of boiling water. Add one teaspoon of salt for every two quarts of greens; boil rapidly about thirty minutes or until tender; drain off the water; chop well and season with butter and salt.

From *The International Jewish Cook Book (1919)*

The Canary
Baked beets and Beet Greens (Tops)

Johnnie Mae was busy cleaning the beets. She had baby CB strapped to her back. That wouldn't last much longer, 'cause he was one load of a toddler, and was wanting to start his walking. The water was boiling on the stove. That told her that the wood fire in the oven was almost hot enough. She would bake the beets and boil the tops. That would be the whole meal. That, and corn bread, fresh made while the beets cooked. No meat tonight. Cletus was sitting at the table drinking the whiskey that should have been their roast beef.

Chow-Chow

Found in *The Cornerpost*

Ingredients
1 peck green tomatoes chopped fine
12 good large onions chopped fine
2 quarts vinegar
2 pounds brown sugar
1 tablespoon of allspice
1 tablespoon of cloves
2 tablespoons of ground mustard
2 tablespoons of black pepper
2 tablespoons of salt
½ teacup grated horseradish

Instructions
Mix all together and stew until perfectly tender, stirring often to prevent burning. Seal in glass jars while hot.

Attributed to Mrs. Septimus Barrow *My Pet Recipes, Tried and True (1900)*

The Cornerpost
Chow-Chow

"Would you like some bread? Our suppers on work days are usually sandwiches."

"Thank you, ma'am, sounds wonderful to me."

Harry plopped a generous spoonful of chow-chow on his plate. "Son, try some of this on your sandwich. Put it top of your meat, not the bread. Gets soggy if you don't." He demonstrated. CB followed suit and took a bite.

"Kinda tastes like souse, what with the vinegar." He licked his lips. "Picklier. I like it." He added more to his plate and loaded his fork. "Good plain, too." He had another bite of the meat and bread, chewing slowly. "Bet this is good on rice."

Harry thought about it. "Probably." He turned to his wife. "Any in the pot?"

"No. We ate it all for dinner." She smiled at her nephew. "Tell us, son, why are you here?"

Cress Salad Sandwiches

Found in *The Cornerpost*

Ingredients
1 cup cleaned watercress
2 or more fresh spring onions
8 slices nice bread, crust removed
Butter for spreading
¼ cup oil and vinegar, mixed for dressing

Instructions
Cress is one of our best spring salads. Pick the leaves over carefully, removing the bruised leaves and all large stems. Mince a young spring onion; strew it over the cress, add a plain dressing. Serve between two slices of bread, crusts removed. Cut the sandwich into triangles to make a dainty.

Adapted from *Fifty Salads (1885)*

The Cornerpost
Cress Salad Sandwiches

Thursday's tea time was a repeat of Wednesday, her back to the rest of the ladies. Louise moved to face the front as soon as the hostess walked away. This time, she ordered tea with best cream and two vanilla sugar lumps, cress sandwiches, and a plate of petit fours, *whatever all that is*. The waitress brought two slices of crust-less bread and butter with the pieces of bitter green weeds between. Just as she was taking a bite of the littlest cake she'd ever seen, a couple strolled past, stopping at the tea room door. "Pha." Louise spat. "I knew it," her snarl muffled by the napkin, "that high and mighty whore."

Cookies & Puddings & Cobblers & Pies

Crybabies

Found in *The Canary*

Ingredients
½ cup lard
½ cup brown or white sugar
½ cup molasses
½ cup raisins
½ cup chopped pecans
1 teaspoon baking soda
½ cup strong hot coffee
½ teaspoon ginger
½ to 1 teaspoon cinnamon
¼ teaspoon salt
2 cups flour

Instructions
Preheat oven between 350-375 degrees. Mix lard, sugar, molasses, raisins and pecans. Dissolve baking soda in the hot coffee and add to batter. Sift dry ingredients and stir into liquid mixture. Drop spoonfuls onto greased cookie sheets.

Bake 12-15 minutes. Let set up 5 minutes before removing from sheet.

(Author's note: Please remember, butter is better.)

Adapted from a collection of recipes from the 1800's submitted by Frances Lindsey and Helen Gravell to *Heritage Cook Book, (author unknown)*.

The Canary
Crybabies

"Jumbles. Plunkets. Crybabies." She turned her call into a plea at the end by saying "cry" just a bit more pathetic and a whine added to "babieeees". The wharf men and sailors would gather with their pennies and she would sell her sweets in nothing flat. How those men loved to look at a respectable widow. Myra would smile, lower her lashes and talk about her children. Sometimes she would speak all their names, listing out Junior, the twins Benjy and Franky, Theo, and Nora Lee. For most of the time, though, she just called them "Babies". The stories really helped with the sales.

Jumbles

Found in *The Canary*

Ingredients
1 cup lard, softened
1 cup sugar
1 egg
1 tablespoon rose water(¾ teaspoon vanilla)
3 cups sifted flour
½ teaspoon salt
½ teaspoon baking soda
½ teaspoon cinnamon
¾ cup raisins
¾ cup large semisweet chocolate chunks
½ chopped pecan
½ sliced almonds
Additional sugar

Instructions
Preheat Oven to 375 degrees F. Sift flour with spices. Set aside. Cream lard and sugar until very light. Add egg and rose water, blending thoroughly. Add dry ingredients all at once to creamed mixture, blending well. Wrap dough and chill in icebox at least 2 hours. On a lightly floured surface, roll out dough to ¼ inch thickness. Cut out circles with a drinking glass. Bake on ungreased cookie sheets 10-12 minutes or until lightly browned around edges. Remove to a rack, sprinkle with sugar, and cool.

Makes about 3 dozen.

(Author's note: Myra used lard because she couldn't afford butter. Butter is better.)

Adapted from *Eliza Leslie's 1857 Cookbook*

The Canary
Jumbles

"Jumbles. Plunkets. Crybabies." The women startled to see Myra approaching them, calling her wares.

"Aunt Ada."

"Sweetheart." *Thank heavens her bonnet was straight and her apron pressed.*

"What are you and the ladies doing out here? Oh, I see Mr. Thomas is with you. Hello, Mr. Thomas. How did your mother like the jumbles you bought for her?"

Plunkets

Found in *The Canary*

Ingredients
1 cup lard
½ cup flour
1 cup sugar
¾ cup cornstarch
6 eggs
2 teaspoons baking powder
1 teaspoon vanilla

Instructions
Cream lard. Add sugar, beating until foamy. Separate eggs. Beat whites until dry. Beat yolk until thick. Pour yolks over whites and gently fold together. Sift twice, flour, cornstarch, and baking powder. Slowly add eggs to creamed lard mixture. Then add dry ingredients and vanilla. Bake in individual greased tins. Use icing if desired.

(Author's note: Bake time and temperature were not recorded. I am suggesting 350 degrees for 10 minutes and then check. Please remember, butter is better.)

Adapted from Janet McKenzie Hill's 1902 cookbook *Practical Cooking and Serving: A complete Manual of How to Select, Prepare, and Serve food*

The Canary
Plunkets

"Well, Mr. Thomas, if it's all right with you, I am going to leave some plunkets on his desk. If he doesn't return today, you make sure the package is taken care of. They might go stale by Monday. We can't let them go to waste." She grinned broadly and so did Mr. Thomas. The young man knew that he and his mama would be having dessert tonight.

Noodle Kugel (Pudding)

Found in *The Cornerpost*

Ingredients
1 pound medium or wide egg noodles cookies and drained
4-5 apples skinned and sliced thin
6 eggs
¾ cup sugar
¾ cup raisins
Pinch of salt
¼ cup orange juice
¼ pound butter

Instructions
Mix all together well. Take ¼ pound butter and melt in 9 by 12 glass pan. Before you pour noodle mix in glass pan, pour melted butter over mixture and combine. Pour noodle mix into glass pan and bake at 375 for 45 minutes. Cut when cool.

Recipe attributed to Ellen Brenner.

The Cornerpost
Noodle Kugel (Pudding)

"Huh?" Louise was startled into attention.

"Oh, don't tell me you don't remember *lokshen kugel*. It is on every Passover plate I know." Esther gave her upper lip a small lick. "*Oy*, so good."

"I'm from Austin. Maybe I know it by another name." *Better watch myself.* Louise looked at the written recipe, reading the ingredients list. "Oh, we called it noodle pudding."

"Well, dear, that is what *some* people call it." Running her finger down the list, Esther stopped at 'raisins', tapping the word with her index finger. "In Brooklyn we used what we could get." She chuckled. "My *bubbe* put in chopped figs one time. We never knew until she told us. Isaac was at that table. Hmmm, maybe you could make it with dried figs. Do you have any?"

Taking that as a cue, Louise stood. "Wonderful idea, I could make this tonight. Have to go to the market tomorrow, anyway. I'll just go a day early. Thank you for coming." She had Esther out the door before the woman had her shawl pinned.

Peach Cobbler

Found in *The Checkerboard*

Ingredients
3 pounds peaches
2 cups sugar
½ teaspoon ground mace (nutmeg)
1 tablespoon cornstarch

Instructions
Line a deep dish with rich thick crust. Pare and cut into halves or quarters some juicy, rather tart peaches; put in sugar, spices and flavoring to taste. Stew slightly and put it in the lined dish.

Cover with thick crust of rich puff pastry and bake until a rich brown color. When done, break up the top crust into small pieces and stir it into the fruit; serve hot or cold.

Other fruits can be used in place of peaches. Currants are best made in this manner: press the currants through a sieve to free it from pips.

To each pint of the pulp put two ounces of crumbed bread and four ounces of sugar. Bake with a rim of puff pastry; serve with cream. White currants may be used instead of red.

(*Author's note:* This cobbler is very palatable without sauce, but more so with plain rich cream or cream sauce, or with a hearty brandy or wine.)

From *The White House Cook Book (1887)*

The Checkerboard
Peach Cobbler

That night Junior went hunting for the men. He found them sitting close by on a pile of rags, eating the same mess Junior just finished. The boy lit his lantern and sat cross legged with them, watching.

Ollie looked up from his plate. "Thanks for the light." He gestured to the food. "Want some?"

Junior shook his head and stared. "How did you two get Cookie's chow?"

"We're thowawayths, but we don't tharve. We paid for thith trip." Jake crumbled his cornbread in his beans and rice so'd he could get all the broth.

Ollie smiled. "I guess we better tell you about us now that we know you are a convicted criminal. Don't want no trouble." He reached behind him and brought out two bowls of peach cobbler. "Sure you don't want some? Good stuff, ya know."

Junior leaned back in the rags. "Had some in mess. How'd you get it?" he asked.

The two men looked at each other and gave a slight nod.

"Black Jack. Him and Sure Foot sneaked us on, and Black Jack feeds us." Ollie was talking with his mouth full. "Yum, these peaches are good."

"What? How? Huh?" Junior's words were gone.

Arabel Gaither's Pecan Pie
Found in *The Checkerboard*

Ingredients
1 cup dark syrup (Arabel used molasses)
½ cup sugar
1 tablespoon flour
1 teaspoon vanilla
2 eggs
¼ teaspoon salt
1 tablespoon melted butter
1 ½ cups pecan pieces

Instructions
Mix and pour in an unbaked pie shell. Bake at 325 degrees for at least an hour until set.

Adapted from Amelia Hofferberth Flory's family recipe

The Checkerboard
Arabel Gaither's Pecan Pie

Annie held out her hand. "Come, my dear, sit back down. We want you to stay." She turned to the head of the table. "Carlton, dear, Princess Dubonet is our guest. Please ask her to return."
"Humph. Sit down, girl, and eat. We will talk about how you can help my wife after pie." He looked around the table. He had no idea which woman baked today. "There is pie, isn't there?"
Arabel nodded, smiling. "Yes Carl, it's pecan, your favorite."
"Pecan must have been your husband's favorite. It's not mine."
"Oh." Arabel started to cry. "Oh."
"Stop that." Emily's tone was cutting. "You don't need to bawl over something as simple as pecan pie."
Arabel cried harder. "You are just jealous because…"
"Sisters, we have a guest. Hush." Annie's admonition brought silence to the room. "I will get the pie. I am sure it will be wonderful."

Fresh Fig Pie

Found in *The Cornerpost*

Ingredients
5 c. peeled figs, cut in half
1 tbsp. cornstarch
7 tbsp. sugar
Juice of ½ lemon
6 tbsp. butter
10 inch lattice-top pastry
1 tsp. cinnamon or apple spice

Instructions
Select figs that are ripe and firm. Place figs in 10 inch unbaked pastry shell. Combine cornstarch, sugar and spice and sprinkle over figs. Add lemon juice and dot with butter. Form lattice top with strips of pastry. Bake in a 425 degree oven for 30 - 40 minutes or until brown.

The Cornerpost
Fresh Fig Pie

Junior returned with two pieces of fig pie. Jack looked at the plates. "Again?"

"Myra says the big shots runnin' LaPorte think fig trees are God's gift to the town. That's why every backyard has 'em. She says we might as well use God's gift."

Jack buried his fork in the back crust. "Did those boss men ever think about what all those seeds do to a man's morning constitutional?" He took a bite and grinned. "They hit me just like raspberries."

"I know what you're sayin'." CB gestured with his fork. "Why you eating your pie backwards? Only makes sense to start at the point." CB dug into his pie the 'right' way.

"My mama always said, 'Boy, bite your crust first. That way, if the fruit's bad, you at least had one taste of the good'." Jack put some of the filling in his mouth, turned and spit it on the grass. "Ugh, that stuff is not fit for man or beast." He went back to the crust. "I know this part is Marguerite's doin'. I can taste the sweet love she puts in it. I'll tell her how good it is."

CB's plate was almost clean. "How you gonna explain that mess of fruit left?"

Jack handed over his dessert. "Won't have to."

Soups & Stews

Julienne Vegetable Soup
Found in *The Checkerboard*

Ingredients
3 onions
3 carrots
3 turnips
1 small cabbage
1 pint tomatoes, stewed
Bunch of sweet herbs (ex: basil, thyme, parsley)
2 tablespoonfuls butter
1 tablespoon flour
Pepper
Salt
1 teaspoon of white sugar
½ cup sweet cream (optional)

Instructions
Chop all the vegetables, except the tomatoes, very fine. Have ready in a porcelain kettle three quarts boiling water; put in all except tomatoes and cabbage, and simmer for one-half hour;.

Add the chopped cabbage and tomatoes (the tomatoes previously stewed); also a bunch of sweet herbs.

Let soup boil for twenty minutes; strain through a sieve, rubbing all the vegetables through.

Take butter and flour; beat to cream. Pepper and salt to taste. Add sugar and sweet cream, if you have it; stir in butter and flour, let it boil up, and it is ready for the table.

Serve with fried bread chips or poached eggs, one in each dish.

Attributed to Mrs. G. A. *Livingston Recipes Tried and True 1894*

The Checkerboard
Julienne Vegetable Soup

After grace, Annie reached for the bell. "We have extra help for this afternoon. First course will be Julienne soup with toast points." Ting, ting. No response from the kitchen. She rang again.

"I'm comin', I'm comin', hold your horses. Give me a minute." The children's voices hushed.

Marguerite's eyes went wide, and she grabbed her husband's hand under the table. "Oh, no, oh no, not here," she mouthed to Jack. She looked at Myra and repeated the silent words. Myra shrugged.

Lulah Marie swung through the kitchen door, a blue willow tureen on her hands. She wore an apron that covered her bright skirts, and her hair twists were pulled up into a black mesh snood.

"Place the soup on the credenza and serve the toast. Thank you." Annie gestured toward the sideboard.

Lulah Marie did as she was told and stepped away from the soup. Marguerite felt a slight tug. One of her pins fell to the floor, releasing a long red braid, leaving the other wrapped around her head.

"Toast?" Lulah Marie asked innocently, offering the plate to Jack. "Missus?"

Chicken Noodle Soup
Found in *The Cornerpost*

Ingredients
4 pounds chicken
2 ½ quarts water
2 ½ teaspoons salt
3 cups cooked noodles
1 teaspoon peppercorns
1 small onion, sliced
1 carrot, sliced
1 bay leaf
1 tablespoon parsley, chopped
Salt and pepper

Instructions
Cut a young stewing chicken into serving pieces, bring to a boil and simmer for 2½ hours, adding water as needed. Skim off the fat and add the peppercorns, onion, carrot, bay leaf, parsley, salt, and pepper. Bring to boil again and add noodles, preferably homemade noodles. Cook for 20 minutes longer.

From *Pennsylvania Dutch Cooking*

Soup Noodles

Ingredients
2 egg yolks
Bit of salt
1 tablespoon cold flour
2½ cups flour

Instructions
Beat the yolks of two eggs with a little salt and one tablespoonful of cold water. Stir in enough flour to make a very stiff dough. Roll out as thin as paper and then roll it up. Let it stand for an hour, and then cut fine with a sharp knife. These will keep any length of time, and can be used in soups, as a vegetable, or in a pudding.

From *The Golden Age Cook Book (1898)*

The Cornerpost
Chicken Noodle Soup

The cooking was almost done when Joe called joyfully from above. "Bring the soup. We have two hungry children to feed."
"Yes sir, will do. I'll carry up our plates and we can have a bedroom banquet." Esther shredded meat on each pile of noodles, and set the tray with silverware, napkins, and bowls. The smell of the soup whetted everyone's appetites.
Isaac slowly fed his son. Ikey asked for some of his father's noodles, but was told he'd have to wait until the doctor came in the morning.

Oyster Stew

Found in *The Canary*

Ingredients
1 quart oysters
4 cups scalded milk
¼ cup butter
½ tablespoon salt
⅛ teaspoon pepper

Instructions
Clean oysters by placing in a colander and pouring over them three-fourths cup cold water. Carefully pick over oysters, reserve liquid, and heat it to boiling point; strain through double cheesecloth, add oysters, and cook until oysters are plump and edges begin to curl. Remove oysters with skimmer, and put in tureen with butter, salt, and pepper. Add oyster liquor, strained a second time, and milk. Serve with oyster crackers.

From *The Boston Cooking School Cook Book (1896)*

The Canary
Oyster Stew

Just then Clarice swung in the back door, leaving the screen open. Behind her was a light skinned colored girl with a basket of oysters.
"You wait here. I'll ask Maude if he wants to cook stew tonight." The girl looked up into the room and blushed, recognizing Jack. After all, not many men had ever tipped their hat to her. Mostly they turned away because of her skin and her reddish hair.
"Comment ca va?"
Jack startled. She spoke like his mama.
"Ca va bien." He didn't know much Louisiana talk, but he did recall the response for 'How are you?' It was the fish gal from the docks, the one with the red hair. She smiled. Jack noticed she had good teeth. He smiled back."Parlez-vous Anglais?" He could only hope because he used up all of his French already.
"Yes." Her cheeks almost matched her hair.
"My name is Jack Smith."
"My name is Marguerite Black."
"Pleased to meet you."
"Same."
The introductions were interrupted by Clarice returning to buy the entire basket of oysters. Marguerite took the money, emptied that basket on the sink sideboard, made a small curtsy, and turned to leave. Jack spoke up.

"I'll look for you on the wharves, if that's all right. Maybe you could teach me some more French?" She made a small nod and left. There just might could be more than stew in his future.

Chicken Stew with Dumplings
Found in *The Cornerpost*

Ingredients
1 chicken or fowl, weighing about 3 pounds
1 tablespoonful of butter
3 tablespoonful of flour
1 large onion
3 slices of carrot
3 slices of turnip
3 pints of boiling water
Salt and pepper

Instructions
Cut the chicken in slices suitable for serving. Wash, and put in a deep stew-pan, add the water, and set on stove to boil.

Finely cut the carrot, turnip and onion, and place into a saucepan, with the butter, cooking slowly for about half an hour, stirring often. Take up the vegetables in a strainer, place the strainer in the stew-pan with the chicken, and dip some of the water into it. Mash the vegetables with the back of a spoon, and rub as much as possible through the strainer.

Now skim two spoonfuls of chicken fat (schmaltz) from the water, and put in the pan in which the vegetables were cooked. When boiling hot, add the three tablespoonfuls of flour. Stir over the fire until a dark brown; then stir it in with the chicken, and simmer until tender. Season well with salt and pepper.

Keep the stew to a simmer. It must not boil hard. About two hours will be needed to cook the chicken. Twelve minutes before serving draw the stew-pan forward, and boil up; then put in the dumplings*, and cook ten minutes.

Take them up, and keep in the heater while you are dishing the chicken into the center of the platter. Afterwards, place the dumplings around the edge. This is a very nice and economical dish, if pains are taken in preparing. One stewed chicken will go farther than two roasted.

*Mix up a batch of biscuit dough and drop by spoonful into the boiling pan (see recipe on page 20, Baking Powder Biscuits).

Adapted from *Miss Parloa's New Cook Book (1880)*

The Cornerpost
Chicken Stew with Dumplings

Noticing the empty room, Mister Charles changed the subject. "Why are you sitting? Looks to me like everybody else is on the floor."

Cocoa lifted the cane hidden under the table. "Sprung my ankle bad. Got took off the floor and put ta washin' dishes. Still gotta stand, but's better 'en not gittin' paid."

"Sorry to hear that. Have you seen Marguerite? Our Miss Girl's somewhere around." He lifted the lid from the ever-present chafer on the side board. "Mmmm, smells good. I'll get me a bowl. You want this old butler to serve you?"

"Thanks, 'preciate it, and yes, I seen her talkin' to Missylou, somethin' 'bout the Bright Star Sisters." Cocoa gestured toward the swinging door. "Don't ya know, that gal grabbed an apron and is out 'ere right now."

The two fell into the rhythm of eating and talking. The chef always heated yesterday's dinner meal for the staff, so if the guests had roast beef with mushrooms on Tuesday, so did they, on Wednesday. This meal was chicken and dumplings.

An hour and a half later, Cocoa was dish washing and the rest of the girls were eating. Sitting next to the still present Mister Charles, Marguerite listened as they told the stories of their day.

Meat & Fish & Eggs

Fried Ham and Pan Gravy

Found in *The Canary*

Ingredients
2 pounds center ham slices cut about ½ to ¾ inch thick
⅓ cup flour
2 cups milk
1 teaspoon sugar
Salt and pepper

Instructions
First, parboil it and drain well. Then fry slices to a light brown, and set aside. Loosen the bits cooked to the bottom of the pan. Make gravy in the same frying pan. Stir the flour into the hot pan scrapings. Add milk, sugar, and salt and pepper to taste. Continue stirring until thick. Pour over the ham.

Adapted from *Recipes Tried and True (1894)*

The Canary
Fried Ham and Pan Gravy

Ike didn't recognize her at first. He was far too interested in his eggs, ham biscuits, and black coffee to pay attention to the breakfast crowd. He always sat at the same corner table so that he could open the Galveston News without bothering anybody. This early morning time alone became a ritual that Ike enjoyed immensely.

"I see you eat ham." The woman was standing beside the table. Her hat was hung down her back, country style, showing wavy brown hair. Her dress was clean but worn, and some of her buttons were replaced. "Ven did you start that? Your Bubbe vould not like."

Pork Chops and Fried Apples
From *The Cornerpost*

Ingredients
6 pork chops cut ½ inch thick
Salt and pepper
1 egg and ¼ cup water made into a wash 4-6 slices stale bread, broken to crumbs
Oil for frying
3 apples peeled, cored, and sliced ⅔ inch thick

Instructions
Season the chops with salt and pepper and a little powdered sage; dip them into bread crumbs. Fry about twenty minutes or until they are golden brown on both sides and tender to cut. Put them on a hot dish; pour off part of the drippings into another pan to make gravy to serve with them, if you choose. Then fry apples in ham skillet. When they are browned on one side and partly cooked, turn them carefully with a spatula, and finish cooking. Dish around the chops or on a separate dish.

Adapted from *The White House Cook Book (1887)*

The Cornerpost
Pork Chops and Fried Apples

Louise didn't show up Tuesday morning. Isaac found a note in the door that read, "Gone to see my mother. Will be back next Monday. PS. Tell Ikey to make his own sandwiches."

That was another thing he didn't know about her. "Wonder if she has a father, sisters or brothers." Isaac looked around the house. "Want to eat at the diner tonight? I don't see anything on the stove."

"Sounds good, can I order pork chops?"

"Yes, Son, I don't know why not." Isaac cricked one side of his mouth. "I remember how tasty they were. Used to have ham biscuits almost every morning with my eggs and grits." He shook his head. "Those were the days."

Ikey wrinkled his brows. "Father, when did you go Jewish? While Mother was alive you were Methodist."

"Grab your cap, boy. I'll tell you about Brooklyn on the way." Isaac tapped his bowler down over his yarmulke. As they walked, he told stories of the tenements and living next to Esther. The two were almost at the diner door when Isaac stopped.

"And to answer your question, I went Jewish at my bris when I was first born."

"Did I have one? Was it a special party? I like parties."

"Son, Jewish follows the mother. She was Gentile."

"So no bris?"

"No bris." *Thank goodness I don't have to explain all that tonight.* Isaac guided his son into that wondrous emporium of smells…and ham. He ordered pot roast and watched Ikey devour his chops. They each had pie for dessert.

Pork Roast with Turnips

Found in *The Cornerpost*

Ingredients
2 pounds pork
1 medium onion cut in wedges
6 large carrots, wedged
6-8 cups water
1 tsp. salt to taste
Pepper to taste
4 lbs turnips, peeled and cut into ½ inch wedge

Instructions
Place the pork and onions in a roasting pan. Add enough water just to cover. Season with salt and pepper. Place on high heat and bring to a boil. Add turnip and carrots and more salt and pepper. Put into a very hot oven until pork is tender, about 1 hour or longer. Remove pork from pot. Taste for seasoning. If the turnips have made the broth bitter, add a bit of sugar before making pan gravy (see recipe on page 105, Fried Ham and Pan Gravy) Serve immediately, or keep over very low heat.

The Cornerpost
Pork Roast with Turnips

He picked up his water glass. "Can I fill yours, too?"

"Thank you. Half full." Ada pulled out the oven rack and slowly lifted the pork roast to the stove top. "My goodness sakes in a bucket, that smells good."

Harry put two topped off glasses on the table and sat back down. "Sure does." He licked his lips. "Would you cut me a taste?"

"No. You know it has to rest to keep the juices in."

"How about a turnip? I'm 'bout starved."

"You are not." Ada forked the juice covered vegetable to a saucer and set it atop Harry's dinner plate. "Here, don't get the meat drippin's on your suit."

"Thank you, ma'am. It looks mighty good." Harry cut into his appetizer. "So, what did Linda Sue do that fired you up?"

"She asked of Myra." Ada felt that covered it all.

"Huh?" Harry chewed on his turnip. "You're all het up over that? Woman, that just don't make sense." He looked hard at her. Her curls were coming loose. "Sit down here and tell me what really is going on."

"Checkin' the rice."

"Sit down right now." Her husband used his 'I've had about enough of this' tone. Ada sat.

She broke into tears. "Flossie Mae's going to hell."

That bit of news sent his most recent bite of turnip across the table. Once the coughing fit subsided, he handed over his breast pocket handkerchief. They both smelled the scorching rice. Harry pointed at his wife. "Do not get up. I'll save it."

The top two inches of the potful was palatable.

Roast Beef
Found in *The Cornerpost*

Ingredients
7-8 pounds rib or loin beef roast
1 cup melted butter (or suet*)
Salt and pepper to taste
1 cup flour, reserving 1 tablespoon
1 cup boiling water
* hard fat found on kidney or loin

Instructions
One very essential point in roasting beef is to have the oven well heated when the beef is first put in; this causes the pores to close up quickly, and prevents the escape of the juices.

Take a rib piece or loin roast of seven or eight pounds. Wipe it thoroughly all over with a clean wet towel. Lay it in a dripping-pan, and baste it well with butter or suet fat. Set it in the oven. Baste it frequently with its own drippings, which will make it brown and tender.

When partly done, season with salt and pepper, as it hardens any meat to salt it when raw, and draws out its juices. Dredge with sifted flour to give it a frothy appearance. It will take a roast of this size about two hours' time to be properly done, leaving the inside a little rare—half an hour less would make the inside quite rare.

Remove the beef to a heated dish, set where it will keep hot; then skim the drippings from all the fat, add a tablespoonful of sifted flour, a little pepper and a teacupful of boiling water.

Boil up once and serve hot in a gravy boat. Some prefer the clear gravy without the thickening. Serve with mustard or grated horseradish and vinegar.

Adapted from *The White House Cook Book (1887)*

Horseradish Sauce

Found in *The Cornerpost*

Ingredients
3 tablespoons grated horseradish root
1 tablespoon vinegar
¼ teaspoon salt
Pinch of cayenne
4 tablespoons heavy cream

Instructions
Mix first four ingredients, and add cream beaten stiff.

From *The Boston Cooking-School Cook Book (1896)*

The Cornerpost
Roast Beef with Horseradish

Nodding agreement, Joe started sliding the red checkers around the board. "Would you be comfortable selling cold meat for sandwiches out of the glass cooler case? Bet the butcher you choose to send people to would be happy to sell you sliced lunch meat as a business exchange."

"I guess I could ask around." Ada humphed. "Harry would have a fit if he knew we were doing that. He was so proud of his meat cutting and those home-cooked roast beef sandwiches he sold."

"Yes, ma'am, they were top notch. Loved the horseradish he used." Joe looked around. "I can see, however, that you and your clerks can't do this alone. You need shelf help. And, my dear, I know just who you can use to help with the books."

To Make Sausages without Skins
Found in *The Cornerpost*

Ingredients
Leg of young pork (uncured hind leg ham)
2 pounds beef suet
2 handfuls sage
2 loaves white bread
2-3 egg yolks
Salt and pepper to taste

Instructions
Take a leg of young Pork, two pound of Beef-suet, two handfuls of Sage, two loaves of white bread, Salt and Pepper to your taste, half the pork, and half the suet, must be very well beat in a stone mortar. Cut the rest of the suet very small; be sure to cut out all the gristles in the pork. When you have mixed these altogether, knead them into a stiff paste with the yolks of two or three eggs, so roll them into sausages.

From *The Compleat Cook (1658)*

The Cornerpost
Sausages without Skins

"Mama, there's somebody at the door."
Theo stood, looking out at a stranger.
"Telegram for Myra Ledbetter."
"It's the telegraph man."
"Hurry," Myra called from the kitchen, "and give him three pennies from the coin bowl. Mixing sausage. Can't come to the door."
Theo made the exchange and brought the missive to his mama. She rinsed her hands and sat down on the stool by the grinder.
MYRA LEDBETTER.
UNCLE HARRY DEAD.
COME NOW.
AUNT ADA.
Myra made into the pantry just before the screams started. She did not come out until there was no voice left.

Souse
Found in *The Checkerboard*

(Author's note: The recipe below is for reading and understanding cooks of that time. Souse can be bought at any fine grocery, packaged under the name head cheese, brawn, or souse. Souse has the most vinegar in it, and makes a delightfully tangy accent.)

Ingredients
Selected pork cuts (feet, ears, nose, heads)

Instructions
Let all the pig pieces you intend to souse remain covered with cold water twelve hours. Then wash them out, wipe off the blood, and put them again in fresh water.

Soak them in this manner, changing the water frequently, and keeping it in a cool place, till the blood is drawn away. Scrape and clean each piece perfectly nice, mix some meal with water, add salt to it, and boil your souse gently, until you can run a straw into the skin with ease.

Do not put too much in the pot, for it will boil to pieces and spoil the appearance. The best way is to boil the feet in one pot, the ears and nose in another, and the heads in a third; these should be boiled till you can take all the bones out; let them get cold, season the insides with pepper, salt, and a little nutmeg; make it in a tight roll, sew it up close in a cloth, and press it lightly.

Mix some more meal and cold water, just enough to look white; add salt, and one-fourth of vinegar; put your souse in different pots, and keep it well covered with this mixture, and closely stopped. It will be necessary to renew this liquor every two or three weeks.

Let your souse get quite cold after boiling, before you put it in the liquor, and be sure to use pale colored vinegar, or the souse will be dark. Some cooks singe the hair from the feet, etcetera, but this destroys the color: good souse will always be white.

From *The Virginia Housewife (1860)*

The Checkerboard
Souse

All were seated and CB handed Jack the meat platters first. Jack did not defer, taking a nice slice each of ham and beef, leaving the cold slices of souse for the others. Myra thought her husband was welcoming their guest. Jack knew CB was honoring the news he brought.

Nora Lee asked for the chow-chow. "Yes'm." Jack passed the jar to the wiggly child beside him. "Missus Myra, where's the rest of your folk?" He made an exaggerated circle with his eyes. "This here table seems to be missin' a boy. Did he get lost somewhere in this fine house?"

"Off to the Island with Uncle Harry and the buildin'. Seems we could all use some help."

Myra patted her bulge. "With you two men headin' back to sea, Aunt Ada will soon be here, bless her. It's going to be very busy with the baby comin'." Just then her dress shifted in front of her. "Goodness child," she said, looking down. "Settle darlin'. Dinner's on its way."

"Mama's baby needs a piece of bread." Theo handed her the basket.

"Yes, darling, we do, and pass some of that good jam, too. The figs are from our tree."

The meal was well appreciated by all. CB had two slices of the souse, loving the vinegar tang. He scraped the last bits onto the other heel and called it dessert. Jack just shook his head. *Crazy white folk, too close to slave slop for me*, he thought to himself. Jam was his dessert. Then Missus Myra stood.

To Cook a Red Snapper
Found in *The Checkerboard*

Ingredients
1 four pound red snapper, scaled, cleaned, deboned
1½ cups buttered bread crumbs
½ cup chopped fresh parsley
⅛ teaspoon each salt, pepper, cayenne, thyme, to taste
1 egg
1 cup water (more if you are planning the gravy)
Basting of butter for gravy

Instructions
Rub the fish with salt, black pepper, and a dust of cayenne, inside and out.

Prepare a stuffing of bread and butter, seasoned with pepper, salt, parsley and thyme; mix an egg in it, fill the fish with this, and sew it up or tie a string round it.

Put it in a deep pan, or oval oven and bake (325 degrees) it as you would a fowl.

To a large fish add half a pint of water; you can add more for the gravy if necessary; dust flour over and baste it with butter.

Any other fresh fish can be baked in the same way. A large one will bake slowly in an hour and a half, small ones in half an hour.

Adapted from *Domestic Cookery, Useful Receipts and Hints to Young Housekeepers*

Cream Sauce for Fish or White Dishes

Found in *The Checkerboard*

Ingredients
⅓ pint of cream
2 ounces of butter
1 teaspoonful of flour
Salt and cayenne to taste
When liked, a small quantity of pounded mace or lemon-juice

Instructions
Put the butter in a very clean saucepan, dredge in the flour, and keep shaking round till the butter is melted. Add the seasoning and cream, and stir the whole till it boils. Let it just simmer for 5 minutes, add either pounded mace or lemon-juice to taste, to give it a flavor.

Time: 5 minutes to simmer.

This sauce may be flavored with very finely shredded shallot or fresh dill.

From *The Book of Household Management (1861)*

The Checkerboard
To Cook a Red Snapper in Dill Sauce

The next course was one of Annie's favorite recipes, poached fish swimming in dill sauce. Lulah Marie had changed aprons, but the snood was forgotten. It was barely clinging to the end of her twists. Once again she walked behind Marguerite. Jack crooked his back his elbow, blocking access to his wife. The fish plate and server were detoured. Lulah Marie side-stepped backwards away from Jack and walked around the table to serve Carlton. As she leaned to offer him some extra sauce, the hair piece fell in the dish. She squawked and dropped the plate, which broke neatly in half. Sauce seeped into the white damask. Lulah Marie Dubonet stared at the mess. The snapper looked fresh netted.

Deviled (Stuffed) Eggs
Found in *The Cornerpost*

Ingredients
6 hard-boiled eggs
½ teaspoon prepared mustard
½ teaspoon tomato catchup (see below)
2 teaspoons soft butter
Salt
Pepper
Paprika

Instructions
Remove shells and cut eggs in half. Mash the yolks to a smooth paste, adding the mustard, butter, salt and pepper. When well mixed, press into the cup-shaped egg whites, round the tops and sprinkle with paprika. For a special treat, add 2 tablespoons finely chopped ham to the egg yolk mixture.

Adapted from *Pennsylvania Dutch Cooking*

Ingredients for common catchup
25 pounds of ripe tomatoes (makes 1 gallon tomato juice)
1 tablespoon salt
1 tablespoon pepper
1 tablespoon cinnamon
1 quart cider vinegar

Instructions

Cut up tomatoes, skins and all; cook thoroughly. When cool, rub through a sieve. To one gallon of tomato juice, put a tablespoonful of salt, one tablespoonful of pepper, one tablespoonful of cinnamon, and one quart of good cider vinegar. Cook until thick.

Attributed to Mrs. F. E. Blake *Recipes Tried and True (1894)*

The Cornerpost
Deviled (Stuffed) Eggs

CLAP. CLAP. Mary stood statue still until she had everyone's ear. "Each family will pack their own main picnic food, and what do you think of each of us bringing a dish to share? I'm pretty good at making stuffed eggs. My mother-in-law's recipe is wonderful." Mary turned this way and that as she talked, noticing how lively the Congress had become. "Is there anyone else in our group who has a favorite family food?" She giggled. "Goodness, we could call the picnic the Favorite Family Food Folderol."

"No, don't use *that* word," said one lady sitting in a corner. "That's their word. Could we call it Favorite Family Food Festival instead?"

About Jacqueline T. Moore

Jacqueline T. Moore works and plays in Murrell's Inlet, South Carolina. She says, "Living in the south makes me a sunflower…and a beach bum!" As a writer and educator, Jacqueline surrounds herself with words. She savors the sounds and sense of letters put together to create a lasting memory. Her debut novel, THE CANARY and its sequel THE CHECKERBOARD are inspired by a most beautiful yellow diamond that rests on her finger and the whispered family secrets about how it got there. THE CORNERPOST is our final visit with Myra, CB and all the children, but if you are hungry for more, take a look at THE CANARY COMPANION COOKBOOK.

Visit her at www.jacqueline-t-moore.com, on Facebook @ Jacqueline T. Moore, and on Instagram @Jacqueline. T. Moore for conversations and updates.

Social Media

Facebook: https://www.facebook.com/pages/Jacqueline-T-Moore/4765684196045

Website: www.jacqueline-t-moore.com

Instagram:
https://www.instagram.com/jacqueline.t.moore

Email: Jacqueline@jacqueline-t-moore.com

Acknowledgements

With deepest appreciation I thank my daughter, Julie Anne Jacobs. Her research is invaluable. I also thank the cooks from the hundreds of years past that practiced and perfected their craft.